Help Your Child To Read

Tell-Tale Tiger

ALLAN AHLBERG and ANDRÉ AMSTUTZ

RAND McNALLY & COMPANY
Chicago · New York · San Francisco

Help Your Child To Read

Parents <u>can</u> help their children to start reading. It is not difficult, nor is it necessary to be a trained teacher. In many ways home is a better place to start than school. In school your child will share the teacher's time with 25 or 30 others. At home your child can have your undivided attention.

The series HELP YOUR CHILD TO READ is a set of books for parents to <u>share</u> with their children. The books contain stories, rhymes and games. Also, on page 3 of each book, there are practical suggestions for parents: ways in which they can help their children to start reading.

Early Experiences

Learning to read begins long before the reading of books at school. It begins with babies and board books; picture books and parents' knees. Gradually young children become acquainted with pictures and print. As time goes by, they get a better understanding of what print is: that it has meaning—it's like talk written down. That it "reads" from left to right, line by line, and top to bottom.

Children need these preliminary skills <u>before</u> they can begin reading. The best time to acquire them is before the age of five; the best place is home—and the best "teachers": members of their own family.

Down in the jungle
living in a tent,
the Tell-Tale Tiger
pays no rent.

But where _is_ he?

Early in the morning
when the sun peeps through,
the Tell-Tale Tiger
peeps through too.

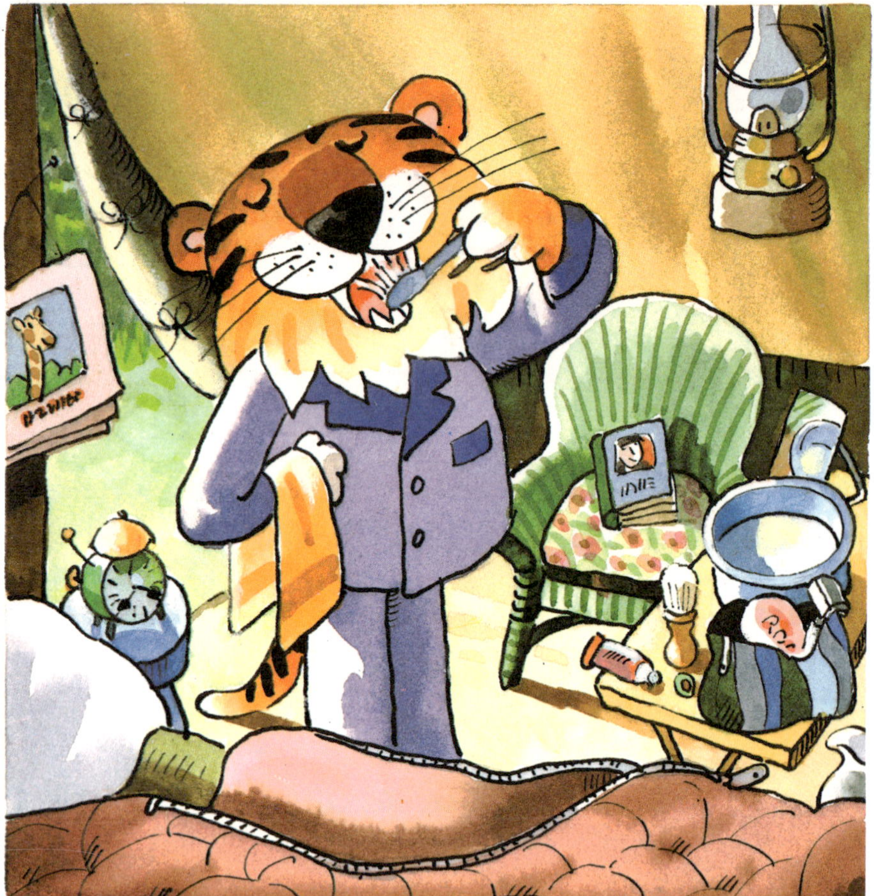

Later in the morning
he carries a stool
to a jungle clearing
green and cool.

What's that book for?

While he wets his whiskers
with ginger beer,
the first little children
begin to appear.

That one's a baby!

The children arrive
from far and wide
and sit in the clearing
side by side.

Now what's going to happen?

Once upon a time...

When he's wiped his whiskers
of ginger ale,
the Tell-Tale Tiger
tells his tale.

That's what the book's for!

It's a tale of teddy bears,
witches and spells,
ghosts and grandmas,
the tiger tells.

Those children are <u>eating</u>!

A tale of giants, boys named Jack,

the Man in the Moon
the Man in Black.

It's not reul though, is it?

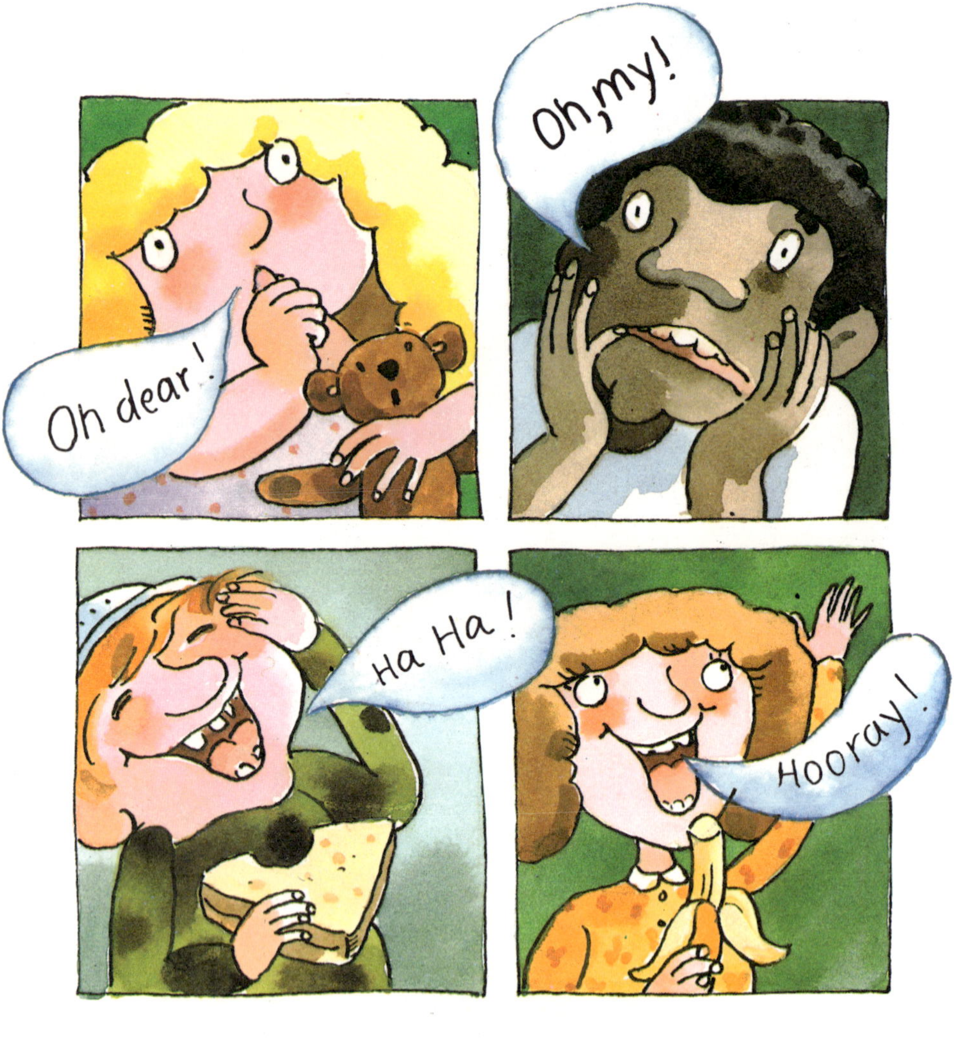
Oh dear!
Oh, my!
Ha Ha!
Hooray!

And the children sit
in a wide-eyed bunch
and smack their lips
and eat their lunch.

Told you they were eating!

When the tale has ended
the children rise.
They stretch their legs
and rub their eyes.

Where's that baby going?

They talk to the tiger.
One strokes his fur.
One sits on his lap.
One calls him Sir!

Now what's going to happen?

Early in the evening
when the sun sinks low,

the sleepy children
homeward go.

Ah—<u>there's</u> the baby!

Later in the evening
as the stars peep through,
the tired tiger
goes home, too.

He could tell himself a tale!

Down in the jungle
sleeping in a tent
the Tell-Tale Tiger
pays no rent.

And is that the end?

Yes!

Tent	Stool
Book	Man in Moon

Grandma	Lamp
Teddy Bear	Baby Buggy

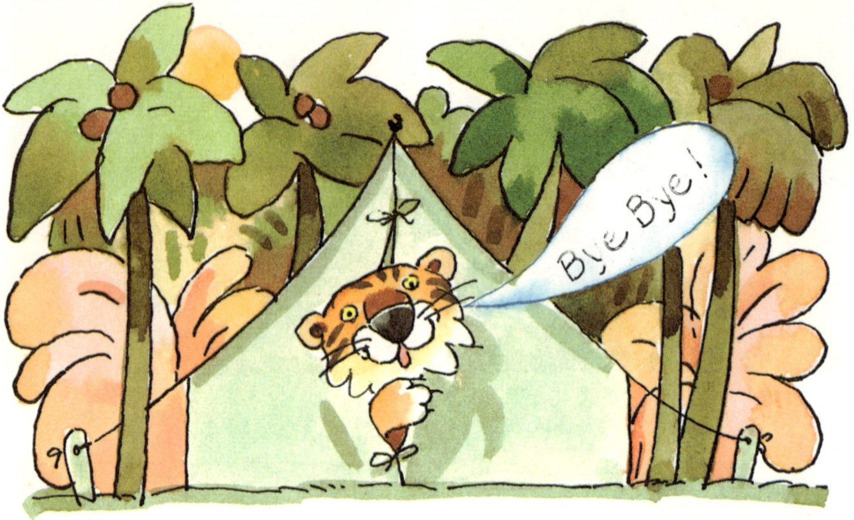
Bye Bye!